THE GOD IN THE RAFTERS

THE GOD IN THE RAFTERS

by

Patrick White

Borealis Press
Ottawa, Canada
1978

Copyright © Patrick White, 1978

All rights reserved. Permission to reproduce any part of this work must be obtained from the publisher.

ISBM 0-919594-97-2

With acknowledgement to Canada Council and the Ontario Arts Council for publication assistance.

Cover design by Joan Rennie.

Borealis Press Limited
9 Ashburn Drive
Ottawa, Canada K2E 6M4

Printed and bound in Canada

Canadian Cataloguing in Publication Data

    White, Patrick, 1948-
       The god in the rafters

    Poems
    ISBN 0-919594-97-2

    I. Title

    PS8595.H428G6   C811'.5'4   C78-000033-1
    PR9199.3W55G6

for JODY and my mother

Contents

Cliff-Jumping	9
Listening for Our Daughter	10
Poet and Dog, Cadboro Bay	11
Morning Glory	12
Mid-Day Moon	13
May 1976	14
Lady in Waiting	16
Our Single Ways	17
Canada Too: Summer '76	18
A Ballad, an Ablution	21
Terrorist	22
Not a Mine, Not a Grave, Not a Hole in the Earth	23
A Little Advice	25
Upon a Gift Going Unused	26
Poetry, My Progress	26
Pai Chu En	27
Words My Grandfather Left Me	35
Verses for the Paradoxical Christians	36
Playing with Jody	37
Confidence	38
Autumn in Ottawa	39
To One "Too Long in City Pent"	39
Glebe Chamber Music	40
Railroads and Waterways	41
For the Astronomers on Little Saanich Mountain	42
Webs	43
One of Four	44
Friday Afternoon	45
Leaves	46
Azazel	47
The Season of True Creation	48
Lampman	49
Winter, Vancouver Island	50
A Fantasy	51

Upon Re-reading an Early Poem of Mine 52
The Rowboat 53
Inscription for the Cairn of an Archaic Indian
   Lying by the Strait of Belle Isle 54
On the Way to University 56
At the Window 57
The Winter Morning Meditation of the Poet-Janitor
   of the Fifth Avenue Free Methodist Church 58
Above Two Capitols 59
Canadian Venus 60
Upon an Old Photograph of Myself 61
In the Parking Lot 62
For Joanne in the Morning 63
The Human Solstice 64
The Premonition 65
Existential Man, the Heredox 66
Skating at Night 67
The Marriage of Heaven and Earth 68
An Attempt at Prayer 69

Cliff-Jumping

To suddenly run right out into barns of air
One moment where you were never meant to be
Then plummet like an angel yielding to space
And land in the soft white sands that slope down to the sea;
Lord, you have lavished great gifts on me.

Listening For Our Daughter

The sleep of a child is of all the perfect peace.
With only a wisp of hair to trouble her
She's warm and safe, the joyful increase
Of parents wide awake if she once stir
A way they haven't heard before, or have,
And know what chore (though they forget whose turn)
Might even rouse them from a quiet grave
(Though I doubt that they could do much more than yearn
I think the habit still might be as strong)
To see what ails a life as dear to them
As any loved a little while or long.
Nor would they put it past her stratagem
As now she wants them up with her at dawn
If sleeping late at last and all the night
She come when dew is fresh upon the lawn
And be to them as welcome as first light.

Poet And Dog, Cadboro Bay

The trim white boats scudding the wrinkled bay
Cruise like gulls against the blue silhouette
Of distant mountains and cold snow;
But it is a beautiful day and warm
And the dog who barks in my ear,
Wanting me to throw his stick
Out to sea, soaking my page
With a shake of his sand and saltwater fur,
Is full of the joy of the chase, is
Vital with an excess of himself.
He spends the day expending in pursuit
Of nothing more than a filthy stick.
He has become the tyrant of the beach,
Demanding each in turn to fling
The object of his doggy soul's commotion,
Or have their eardrums broken for the breach.

Victoria

Morning Glory
for Michael Best

And though I work to rid the garden of it,
(Rows of empirical carrots, rational radishes,
Facts like stepping stones throughout the patch)
I've come to respect its strange tenacity,
Its wayward way of sprouting here and there.
Chop as I may at its roots with a spade,
Though I hack like Alexander at his knot,
Yet it will grow again two days from now,
Unfurl its pale green leaf, exact its space
Among the vegetables and cultivated herbs.
It grows in spite of all my labour,
Wound tight about the garden-stakes
I'd meant for beans, constrictive helix
Coiling like a fundamental molecule,
Its chlorophyl ascending stairways to the sun,
It grows to grow, no other purpose set;
Roots deep in radical conspiracies,
Its leaves attempt to climb to power
Upon the backs of lesser, weaker plants
Whose usefulness will always see them spared.
But for that (and only that) I'd let this hardy have its way,
I'd leave the garden to its own affairs
And judge that worthiest which could prevail,
Nature letting nothing stand it did not mean.
I would not stoop, as now, to pull this green enthusiast
From soil enriched by years of care and privilege;
I'd turn my garden back to equal opportunity
And let the fancy lettuce, dill, and beans
Contend without my help against a weed
Whose one offense is overwhelming life.
I'd watch its trumpets raise their senets to the sun,
And like a tired Roman know an empire over-run.

Mid-Day Moon

Ghostly crescent rising on my thumb-nail,
I see you up there in your pale acres
And wonder what influence you wield
When lovely girls undo their bras
And lie down upon the glaring sand
In rows, to darken in the sun;
I wonder what has roused you to that height
When there seems to be so little call
For the darker agents of your light.

May 1976

1.

Just before the lilac starts to wilt,
I name these beautiful things:
Lilac, sparrow, snowbird,
And even the wallflowers by the white fence,
Glorifying rust, intensifying gold,
I name them with all the rest
Before caterpillars are full-grown
On bloom, on leaf, on bole;
And then I name the caterpillars
As summer turns its Assyrians loose on the fold.

2.

Let's prepare a volume for spring.
Let's sit down like a gay Rasputin
And see into the dark heart of things.
O let's let go of the bloody crucifix
That squanders simple, lovely things,
Let's tear down those gruesome sticks,
Let's thrust them in the ground and tie strings
Between. Let's come to flower like a bean
And tempt our own perishing;
O let's come down like pagans
On the Central Asian Plains!

3.

Reek of lilac in the air,
I feel the wild daughters egging me on;
I see the lustre of red-enamelled fingernails
That would walk my back like brittle crabs;
I spread my hand upon a soft rocking pelvis
That swells like a melon
And divine the life to come.

4.

Raw, naked bulb. Blunt bolt. My cock.
Let's address you in the open;
Let's commit a decent exposure.
Soft Vesuvius of warm white snow,
Let the liars sublimate in the towns below:
Morality is slag.
Go for their daughters!

5.

All women are Sabine
When Rome rips off their skirts:
Women are basically imperial,
Their talons wedged into the timeless enterprise
That bears them like a bloody standard
Into history.

6.

Rome must also be thought of as a violet
Simmering in the dark heat
Of a May afternoon;
Or the ghostly pink
Of a florid rhododendron
That takes your breath away
Until you notice the Japanese quince
Colour of scalded shrimp
And suddenly you are lifted up
Like a lake of hot flamingoes.

7.

Appalled by Rome,
Now let the daughters of Rome
Be appalled in the tents of the Pagan.

8.

There's matter for a theme.

Lady In Waiting

Now pass the rhododendron, lilac, plum,
As there in the shade of the fence
The rich royal peonies come,
Their globes like massive planets.
A little too rich for my blood,
That plush extravagant bloom;
And all for a bee, is it possible?—
I back off with the rest to make room.

Our Single Ways

There seemed to be no birds among the trees
Though high up here and there a gull
Circled on a thermal, or shot the breeze.
It was his turn to push as it was mine to pull.

The old abandoned pipeline road,
A ribbon of red clay through miles of wood,
Was bracken either side, the colour of toad,
But it was the lack of birds that changed our mood

And made us chat the louder as if to say
We didn't realize the land was anyone's
And if we had, we wouldn't talk this way,
But try to steal across as innocent as nuns.

We acted like two players in a play
Who were in fact two frightened railwaymen.
I was certain we hadn't come a way
That seemed with every step a little more forbidden

But he insisted that O yes we had
And probably because he was the senior hand
I went along awhile with what he said
And wasn't bothered by his reprimand.

Though I had been lost before and so had he
We had never been lost with another
Who had each other then for company
So if we were lost we were lost together.

Though neither ever said, nor would,
I think we preferred to be lost alone,
But lest we be misunderstood
We kept this thought an undertone;

So it was his turn to pull and mine to push
As we strained to keep on with a load
Either alone would have left to the bush
And gone our single ways upon the same uncertain road.

Canada Too: Summer '76

The emperor's elder sister,
Getting on in years,
More evergreen than deciduous?
No more than a cigarette
Tucked behind the ear
Of the executive to the south;
One hand on her frozen knee?
She is unwieldy as a glacier
Withdrawing north.
Ice-sphinx raking its claws
Deep into granite, she knows
The slow, slow ecstasy
Of rising mountains
Where owls wait for the moon.
Governed by retired majors,
She lets her desires loose
Like shy cougars
That swim across in the night
To startle the downtown drunks.
She is huge, tapering off
Into the baffling Socratic clarity
Of a North
That troubles her like a conscience.
She can teach a man to survive,
Or craze him with gold, with ores,
With oil that oozes up out of her
Like wine from crushed grapes.
Country of good poets
And better pilots,
She gives up baby mammoths
To archaeologists and wolves;
Her keepsakes
Are the nails of Viking villages,
Mysterious scored bones,

Miles of Cariboo fences.
She is a Gargantuan overestimation
Untried by a Napoleon, a Hitler;
She is a potential tyrant-tamer,
An unconquerable pantry.
Her museums are full
Of dying native cultures.
She has one channel,
And two languages;
She has avoided declarations.
She had a doctor named Bethune.
Her businessmen are no better,
Her politicians no worse.
She likes to detect submarines
From the air.
She has no Indian air marshals
Or Eskimo admirals.
She has three banks in Barbados
And a number of satellites in space.
She wakes up,
Spreads marmalade on her toast,
Pours canned milk on her porridge.
She has her own branch
Of the Oxford University Press.
She is waiting,
Or has she waited long enough?
Germans, Japanese
Grope toward her other knee;
She does not own Toronto.
Her railways lose money.
She holds her secrets close to her
Like Franklins;
She is as mysterious
As Tom Thomson's overturned canoe.
She relents
With an Emily Carr.

If she dresses up
It's Montreal; if not?—
Timmins, Terrace, Grand Prairie.
She has pretty postage,
And a two dollar bill
The colour of water in old coffee-cans.
She has a quick unsatisfying summer
And a fall
To blacken strawberries on a hillside.
She's fabulous for leaves.
Catullus would have preferred Sirmio
But she is as big
As the Roman Empire.
Her poets are making leagues,
Her soldiers humus
At Vimy, Dieppe, P'an Luc.
She is remembered fondly
By the Dutch
And has business connections
In Cuba, in South America.
She is seldom kidnapped,
But she is expecting
Trouble at the Olympics,
A gold medal in dressage.
She is not Sappho,
But if a whale is washed up
On either of her shores,
Some few will kill it,
Some few will write volumes.

A Ballad, An Ablution

She

You did not use to hesitate so;
You did not use to come near me
With your stale breath and unwashed body;
You did not use to treat me so.

He

You did not use to let me see,
You did not use to let me know
How moles and freckles and pimples all grow
On you, as see?— they grow on me.

Chorus

They did not use to notice such things,
They did not use to care;
They were a loving, lusty, poreless pair
Who bathed together and left no rings.

Terrorist

All the parts were there, the plan was good,
It was, I had to admit,
A masterwork of detail;
(I read his poem like the blueprint of a bomb).
And yes, its main antipathy was right,
Its trigger had the instincts of a snake.
Its prime objectives?—
To play with matches in the summer timber,
To put a scorpion in every shoe;
To steal some portion of the holocaust
And deliver it like a poisonous orchid
After the singing telegram.
And yes, I thought, this poet
Stares out of his poem
Like the baked eye of a radioactive lizard.
He could razor a baby
If the cause were right; his heart
Wired to bad philosophy
Like a clock in an airport locker.
As it is, he has learned to use the mail.

Not A Mine, Not A Grave, Not A Hole In The Earth
for Mike Doyle

There is a certain grey light to a basement
I have often associated with the truth;
An honest look to the unfrosted globe's bright filament,
And the easing odour of damp black earth.

Here is the sickle that rusted years ago,
Still balanced on its crooked nail, an edge
Enfeebled as the hand that's forgotten how
To use it, or axe, or hoe, or blunted wedge

That split the cedar lengths with a crack
Into muscular rivers of auburn wood;
And here are some eggs of coal in a sack,
And here, greasy fingerprints on an April nude;

And there is the hammer with only one claw,
And there, six feet of aging barracuda,
Is the wide rip-toothed two-handled saw
That gripped and buckled in the green sitka

When men worked in rhythm with their feet apart.
Here are tools as fit for the tomb of a pharoah
As any trinket struck by Egyptian art;
Here rasping mowers dream of laying the new blades low.

And is this not also where summer's grapes ferment
And potatoes put out their eyes;
And is this not the place of the death of paint
That grows thick-skinned as it dies?

Here is a jar of bent nails someone never used,
Of washers, bolts, a faucet's rubber rings,
And here is where the leftover poisons are housed
That killed the rat and robbed the caterpillar of its wings.

A low world of forgotten purposes and castaways
Where the spiders are silently eating
And no one entertains; no one prays;
And no one comes down with a ready greeting.

A world of hideous incident and slow foreboding,
And yet a child can play here for hours alone;
A world where the circuits are overloading
And the pipes give a shake then let out a groan.

Not a mine, not a grave, not a hole in the earth,
Nor yet a place for laughter;
Not a womb, not a tomb, though the cat gives birth;
Nor yet a place to ignore the god in the rafters.

A Little Advice

If you would be free of suffering,
Give it a name, draw
Analogies, propose, if you must,
Some little drama to act out in;
Set the whole turbulence of self
Against self; like the god
Of the old romance,
Be a storm, amass, overwhelm,
Grow huge and rise, rise
Against the rational skylines you did not invent.
In every man
Is original Promethean fire, in
Every man is a Spartan thief; rise
Who are sleeping in ashes, rise
And ascend the laughing scaffolds of yourself;
Be eloquent, brief,
And when the floor finally yields, drop,
The last, most cunning of lures.

Upon A Gift Going Unused

Its strings are as tight as a runner's tendons,
Its wood echoes to the drum of idle fingers,
The talk talk that booms from jungle logs
As a single ignorant plucked note lingers,
Pleasing the beast who plays the red guitar
Or holds it humming in the hollow of its shell
Like a boy with a bee in a canning jar.
But most of the time in its case in the corner
It leans against the enduring wall,
Propped like a sprinter set to go;
There where the lean Segovian spiders crawl,
It stands like a dead tree in fields of snow;
Come, all who would, pick it up and play,
And be the genius of a happy, skillful day.

Poetry, My Progress

I came to it as an ant to a Venus fly-trap,
Attracted by the reek of dewy sap.
I am (I still contend) an ant;
But it behaves oddly for a plant.

Pai Chu En

Presented by Canadian artists as a gift to the Chinese People's Republic in 1976 and is presently in the care of the Norman Bethune Medical Centre in Shih Chia Chuang.

Early June and the rain is as warm as the blood
That stains his hands
And mingles with the sweat on his eyelids
As he tries to rub the weariness away. O Frances
For a moment there he thinks
But she is years gone and here before him now
Is all he knows. O Frances
The human body is a deep well
Of soft wet . . . but the image fades . . .
More light, more light, more bloody light!

His hands move like spiders working at a web.
Incision made, fat parted,
In go his hands, bare
Because you would not stroke a girl
With gloves on, and Life,
I assure you, is Feminine, and then
The sounder reason, the Scottish heritage:
I can feel more with the gloves off.
I am more sensitive with the gloves off,
And an artist needs to be sensitive,
And I am an artist!— It saved lives, it
Saved many many lives, it
Was a man until 1939 whereupon
It left the broken body of Norman Bethune.

O Frances your body was a deep well
Where I used to call out my name
And hear in the summer dark
My name resounding. Frances, did I say
I loved you, did I ever say
I loved you girl? (Yes dear,
Many times.)

Early June and the rain is as warm as the blood
That stains his hands. A young Chinese
Or is it Spanish soldier
Dies on the door he was
Brought in on. The sound of rain
Is insufferable against the corrugated tin roof
Of the makeshift theatre.
The earth steams like hot soup
And the salt of his own sweat is in his eyes.

For you, my dearest Frances,
Partly for you I
Am a martyr now to a race
Not my own, in a country not mine,
Among a people where I came to peace.
Here, Frances, here, my monument,
Second only to Mao's.

Another body on a stretcher appears before him.
The wound is alive with maggots.
Infection. Shock. The world is wrong.
He picks the worms out one by one
With tweezers. The world is wrong.
Easy, son, easy. Almost done.
But the worms have already begun.

He shuts the boy's eyelids.

Why must so many die, why any at all
Continually, why when the rains
Are flooding the paddies with warm lush life
Must death gape like an open mouth
Brimming with its own blood?
Take it away. Take it away.
My sinuses are rife with the smell, my eyes
Glazed with the sight, my hands
Numb with the work. Take it away!

God's work, Frances, I am doing God's work,
And at the same time helping the General
And myself, and you, and these people, Frances.
I know they need me. I know I am needed, Frances.

Early June and the rain is as warm as the blood
That stains his hands. Needed—
That is why he is here, why
It is his thumb and forefinger
Pinching off the severed artery
Of the young Chinese or is it Spanish soldier.

He watches the peasant children
Trying to catch frogs
In the warm, summer rain. What hope
Can be held out for them who will
Never sow
Or harvest a crop, who must now
In the trampled paddies of their dead father
Fight each other to dip their tongue
In the cold blood
Of a frog? What hope
Can be given to them like a small bit of wax
To chew on in the night
When they wake, and they're hungry,
And they ask you where their parents are,
And you know?
      A leg, an arm,
An eye ruptured by stray shrapnel, a life;
What difference does it make anymore?
I have run a saw through more bone
Than I ever did trees in the bush back home. Home? . . .
And where might that be but where
I am needed?—O Frances
It has become so difficult without you.

But I am of a line
Of strong, violent men
God has made cruel with the truth, with
A vision of unworthiness, of worth, and I say
Maggots have an easier time than men in the world, men
Are their markets,
Like the doctors back home
Taught how to heal for money, how to quell
The palpitating heart
For a dollar, how to bind
The blasted stump of the child
Who tripped the forgotten mine
For a dollar, for a dollar
Let out like a hem the rich fat of the hog
Who buys the skill of a man who can heal while
Maggots staunch the wound
Of the young Chinese or is it Spanish soldier
Dying for the lack of doctor, of a dollar,
Quietly, softly, like so many other times
When no one was looking, when the world
Was busy with its affairs
When neither mother nor father nor wife nor son
Were thinking of where he might be
When even the flies
Seemed busy otherwhere
One dark humid afternoon
The young Chinese or was it Spanish soldier
Felt his colon relax and life slip out of him
As easily as he fouled himself
And knew it was the last humiliation.

I wait for the ascendant man for whom
Thought is a bloodless ritual, a moving on
Over the years away from mutual slaughter,
The ruptured kidney, the gangrenous arm.
Thought is the violence of evolving men.
There is more of the jungle in Mao

Than Christ, more in Christ
Than Plato. Thought,
The more scrupulous predator,
The violence of evolving men
Constrained to help
Because that is most difficult.

Early June and the rain is as warm as the blood
That stains his hands.
And there is nothing to kill the pain
Of the maimed idealist dying in agony
Because the rain has turned the road to mud
And the truck is stalled.
No anaesthetics,
Be strong for Mao,
The Proletariat, the Cause. No anaesthetics,
Bite down hard on the Revolution like a bullet.
Make of death
A good example
Though no one know your name
And you have no sandals, die
Better than the Japanese,
Better than the Kuomintang, die
Like hope on the incredulous doctor's face.

Almeira, Malaga,
How many thousand miles away, and who
Was the hero there, who
The right man to follow?
He remembered the constant raids,
The civilian targets, the Stukas testing their bomb racks
On children, old women, all
Huddled in crumbling doorways, praying
Praying, always praying,
And who could tell if it did any good?

The panzers that should have been beaten into ploughshares,
The Messerschmidts strafing the refugee lines,

The machine-guns with new cooling systems—
The future had opened like a toybox.
Civilian targets, the weakest link,
He could remember the smell of scorched dog
And worse. War was a morbid painter,
Like himself, delivered once
As he was in a painting
By the Angel of Death
To what greater life, what greater glory won?—
As he could almost wholly believe.

Manchuria, Hopei, Japan, China, Spain,
Italians, Fascists, Nazis, Socialists,
Capitalists, Nationalists, Anarchists,
Kuomintang, Imperialists, Christians,
Buddhists, Catholics, Protestants,
Canadians, Americans, and then the People
Who died in the name of none of these,
The endless thousands,
While lunch is taken in Gravenhurst,
While all that over there is going on,
Would anyone believe who's dying in my arms?

Someone gave a dollar.
He wrote a medical text.
Someone gave a dollar.
He invented a new surgical instrument.
Someone gave a dollar.
He built a hospital.
Someone gave a dollar.
He organized mobile blood transfusion units.
Someone gave a dollar.
He waived his fee for a poor patient.
Someone gave a dollar.
He worked nineteen hours a day.
Someone gave a dollar.
He gave his rations to the needy.

Someone gave a dollar.
He rebuilt the hospital.
Someone gave a dollar.
He laid down his life

And in 1971
The National Historic Sites and Monuments Board
Declared he was not qualified to be
A Canadian of National Historic Significance;
And then a wheat deal with China went through
And suddenly, he was.

Early June and the rain is as warm as the blood
That stains his hands. The scalpel
Slips. He cuts his finger.
One moment to bandage it
Then back to work, but
It is not until the soldier with the infected, fractured skull
Is examined routinely
That a cut like this one
Will take on any significance: Septicaemia,
Resulting in death.

Pai Chu En
On a white horse,
A gift from General Nieh,
Taken from the Japanese.
Pai Chu En
On a white horse, Frances,
Crossing the Wu-t'ai Mountains,
Norman Bethune from Gravenhurst!

And then he was deaf.
And then he was dead.

No Red Ensign, no Union Jack,
He was buried in the next best thing:
The Chinese laid him out in the Stars and Stripes.

What could he say
To make us think
It mattered?

Words My Grandfather Left Me

I have asked after my life on the planet,
This brief embassy from the mud;
I have gazed long at Orion's stars,
Turned rocks at the edge of the sea;
In bracken up to my knees
In an ancient cedar forest,
I have put my question to the trees
And heard high up in their boughs
Only the vague oceans of the breeze;
Or from blue Rigel's trembling light,
Only the hiss of interstellar waves
Till I must think that heaven raves;
But I have put my question right.
In the highest galleries of the house
My voice has struck the ears of those
Behind a darkness born of light;
I've raised my issue on their floor,
Chose matter, mastered terms, strange lore,
Anything to help me frame it right.
In language pure and strong
As old oak in a right arm,
I've gone and pounded on the door
As if hell could be raised to alarm,
Earth praised by a plain song,
Or heaven won by a lack of charm;
Yet have I gone right up like Luther to the door
And dared the beating heart within to say
What all my blessèd hammering was for?

Verses For The Paradoxical Christians

Lay it down, brother, brick by brick,
For we're building a temple at Nazareth,
For we've seen a light that bids us build,
For the light of the Lord is an aftermath,
For the light of the Lord is a joyous guild
Say the sons of the Lord Arch-Heretic.

Soft as the powder on the wings of a moth
As gentle, He, my sister, sing,
For we're working a loom in the Lord's own house,
For the lawn of the Lord is a night-moth's wing,
For we're mending the fold of moth and mouse
Sing the sisters who patch the Lord's Whole Cloth.

Playing With Jody

I am a train
Rubbing my shoes on the nylon carpet
As I touch the nose of my laughing daughter
And a little spark
               jumps
With a shock   jumps
With a delicate click of bluish light
As I aim at her nose and the lobe of her ear
To hear the joy in the laughter
               O God
To tempt tears
As I hold out my finger
Like Adam from the Sistine Chapel Roof
And hear the joy in the laughter
As click click click
               I go crazy
Firing off
God's subatomic cap-gun
                   again and again
As whole and laughing
She drops to the floor,
Riddled with life,
My daughter.

Confidence

He thinks because he's good,
Because he has his youth, a girl, his mind,
It will all come out right in the end;
He need only wait until a committee's formed
To once and for all
Winnow the grain from the chaff;
Himself, of course, "richly garnered",
(His girl an asset in a tight fix).

I think of Mozart, that lonely man,
Looking up at the ceiling of another strange room
As death mauled his greatness
Like a bleating judas-goat;
He took Vienna like a late spring,
Maestro of its swallows! And yet
Few would wish to meet his end;
Few would wish to share his gift,
Knowing as they do what worst befell
The prodigy, the genius, the man
Who had for his reward
A trussed-up virgin's expletives,
A sense of what was dying with him,
And a view as he stared at the ceiling
Of only the ceiling. Poor Mozart,
Did he forget for a moment how to win;
Distracted from the world a moment by a theme,
Did he not see the malignant boys
Slowly gather round the beautiful monarch butterfly
They hosed off the Queen Anne's Lace
And drove into the mud with their pee?

It isn't going to happen to him,
This bastard swears,
Doing up his fly.

Autumn In Ottawa

High and wild among the trees,
Mad Herod of the leaves
Swept into a great eddying pell-mell,
Goes the wind as it reaves
Even the tattered clinging few
Whose stems are tougher than sinew
In the late October air
Now leaves are brown and dry
And crack like old Van Dykes;
Goes the wind on its timeless way
As cloud and sun contend
In the heart as well as the eye
Of the whole scene's lone beholder;
Goes the wind through the sky today
Like a crazed man through a folder.

To One "Too Long In City Pent"

There is life between the bricks, pale roots
With leaves like tiny ears,
Searching for shy illusive photons;
And in coming years
Long after you are dead,
Grass will still break cement like bread.

Glebe Chamber Music

A cold wind clamors at the windowpane,
Whistles over the hollow of the chimney-pot
Like a whiskey-jug, then dies down again,
Receding into the night like some mournful train;
When suddenly sheet-metal ducts unknot
And the furnace starts up with a stadium's roar
To give even these old red bricks a shake
And startle the ghosts in the walls awake;
So all night long I hear them walk the floor,
Whole companies pacing the creaking board
While the mice in the garbage beneath the sink
Make up another no less noisy horde
As bottle and tin now strike their chord
Though a little late, that antiphonal clink.

Railroads And Waterways

The freezing air now takes a life-mask of my face
And leaves are thatched under thin snow
Like old biblical fire in the heart
Of a young evangelist. Soon every path
Will make ordeals of balance; soon
Ice will make all paths impossible,
But let that be; I think of home,
Walking here beside the still canal
Where the willows lean out to wash their hair
Like my sisters under a kitchen tap.
A vision of grey, soft, winter days
Wells up before me like the mist
That hangs suspended in the air
And leaves upon a woollen sleeve
A billion, perfect, gleaming spheres.
And I grow sad to think I am not there,
And try, by picking up my pace,
To stay the gentle execution of my tears;
Then half overcome by the emotion,
Smile to think if anyone should see,
Thus weeping beside a canal for an ocean,
The latest consequence of running
A railroad out to beautiful, far B.C.

Ottawa 1976

For The Astronomers On Little Saanich Mountain

I remember those cold nights
I walked down the mountain
From the observatory
With all creation's stars in view
Through the black pines.
I had the earth to myself,
I was Adam, satisfied,
Gazing up at the notions of God
As if my eyes were filled with wine.

Webs

For weeks it fattened on the moths and flies
That toiled against the windowpane;
It grew as plump as any banker's wife,
Though what it did was not for gain,
Nor even out of malice for the frantic life
That saw itself in all eight eyes
As the spider reared, bit, then secured its prize.

Nor was there malice in my fast heart
When I steeled myself to the act;
Life, I said, is to be accepted,
And I entered into a silent pact
With a killer nature perfected.
If I must plead for this black part,
Then let my plea, I thought, be Art.

Thus I let the spider stay,
Tucked in a corner of the windowsill,
And I watched as it sprang at the tug of a strand
And ran like a pianist's hands to kill;
Then I saw the slow drip of its poisonous gland
As it seized its fluttering prey;
And then I winced to feel my own skin give way!

Out, then, out with the hideous thing,
And I flung it in the grass outside:
I'll give the moths and flies a chance
I thought, and wiped the sill of webs, dry-eyed;
For the fate of a spider was fixed in my glance
Far back in the mind's beginning
When I, too, woke to the first faint tug on a string.

One Of Four

I keep looking at the lawn with its autumn leaves
And the long black shadows of the trees across it.
An earthy sweetness rises from it this October,
Recalling the generations of man that are sod.
It is possessed of an old world beauty
Like a suede-bound volume of verse;
And in the late afternoon when the air
Is temperate and still, with only a falling leaf, perhaps,
To say the scene is not some lonely woman's watercolour,
It is a more profound symbol of the mystery of life
Than the sea, or the stars, or the wind.

Friday Afternoon

I hear the shrieks of the children coming home from school
All in a gang, and I think
How they are the envy of the birds
Who sit in silence on the wires above
And wish for something very much like words.
And there, that one in the red, is my daughter,
Beginning to lead a life of her own;
For now I too sit in silence at a window above
Without words to express the love
Or the loneliness I feel
Knowing what other men must have known:
There is in the sight of a child coming home from school
That which makes us speechless and wise
And that which calls us loquacious, and fool;
But deeper than either of these
Is that which would have me down on my knees,
Thanking any remote god, however far,
With the highest praise my heart bestows: You are.

Leaves

Singly drop the shadows down the sunlit wall
Of leaves like passing images in Plato's cave;
So God shakes the tree of yet another fall
And dark wings tumble to an earthly grave.
I lie my book upon my lap and try to read
Transient ciphers dark in the glowing light
Squared by the pane to a page outspread
Whereon must God dissemble in our sight;
For we know the world by light forbidden to us,
Held back in the heart of matter and mind
Like the shadows of leaves there falling across
A bright wall set before mankind;
We seek the undelivered secret of the light,
Which is God restraining to blind our eyes;
We look up, impaired as we are in sight,
And peer at the shadows of shedding trees;
And know by the tempered light of the leaves
That are falling down the opposite wall,
How for his creature the Lord God grieves;
That the Lord God grieves for his creature at all.

Azazel

Angel in the tree, poet
Locked in heartwood,
In the dark of summer storm
I have seen your great vans
Rail heaven with anger and praise,
I have seen your head incline to earth,
As if you swanned before the block,
Arms or wings outspread,
And God were an imported
French executioner, hawkish,
Hooded, but for the eyes,
Begging forgiveness even as
He rouses the lightning above
To cleave you through the nape!

The Season Of True Creation

A cold October rain saturates
The leaves that were only yesterday adrift
Like a drunken pilgrimage upon the giddy air
Of their first unleaving. Autumn's lustrates,
They were given up freely then, a parting gift
To the wind that delights to scatter them everywhere
Like a fleet Saracen the Christian hordes
That fled before the gleaming ripple of his knife.
And so I am reminded how it is with words
That set out, perhaps, to resolve some alien strife
Simply on the strength of their pure and faithful going,
Like winding miles of children singing hymns
To the glory of God, Omnipotent, All-Knowing,
Who knows a parent by these wet, black limbs.

Lampman

Under the burning maple at the pond's edge,
Effortless as mercury on glass,
Glide two huge swans and their cygnet,
A triple wake within a moving wedge,
As sunlight deepens to an older brass
Like the lines of the fatally stricken poet
Whose ghost is held a tenant of the time;
For now more manifest than my imaginings,
Some resident spirit in the late sublime,
Lingering on those folded wings,
Presages soon they must be spread
And following their constellation down:
His spirit seems this tardiness of light,
His spirit here delinquent from the dead,
And still delays though dark is coming on,
And stays to be the first star out tonight.

Winter, Vancouver Island

The Dipper's bowl was full of lighter, swifter cloud
After the rain had exhausted itself;
And that was all this winter had in store
It seemed, all it had upon its shelf,
Despite the children wishing hard for snow.
Once again the island kept to green,
Faithful to the colour of things that grow.
Shower after shower came and went
As wish upon wish was silently made;
But there was never a flake, not the slightest hint
Of anything white but the clouds above.
Nor were there only children at the windowpane,
But adults, too, to take it for a sign of love
If winter'd only once done something cold to rain.

A Fantasy

Between the double
Windows of the half-double,
Swung like the cables
Of Golden Gate,
A spider's drawn his web;
A thousand strands perhaps
Swept up like snow against the sill.
It makes the place look Christmasey
In a macabre way;
An eerie snowbank gleaming
In the streetlight.
But not the cold of snow
I pack about my heart,
Dreaming of the thing sometimes,
Fascinated by its treachery
As light limns each
Pliant strand like the cables
On the deck of a ghostly aircraft carrier
Sweeping through the night,
Looking for its overdue
Squadrons. Not
The cold of snow.

Upon Re-Reading An Early Poem Of Mine

The wind is in the leaves like a young tide
Rocking itself into crushing swells.
Not wholly at play, it seems to test
Its strength against the swinging boughs;
For there's Achilles wading through the Trojan plain,
His arm not yet heavy with the loss of his friend,
Nor death let its pollen to the wielding wind.
He exerts himself in gusts, each
A little stronger till one by one
Leaves and cowardly captains break and run;
But then behold the holocaust when armies flee
And mad Cassandra raves upon the walls!
Then can you see what I see, my friend:
Young tides and poets in those squalls?
Do we look up into the same stricken tree?

The Rowboat

Walking along the Rideau canal this windy dusk,
An undulating collage of autumn leaves
Upon its black water, I found a rowboat
Drifting, wholly-submerged, but still afloat,
And for a moment took fright someone was hurt
And braced myself to find a corpse nearby,
But finding nothing, was satisfied at last
The boat had simply slipped its mooring in the night.
Thereupon I saw in it the image of a heart
Drifting slowly without oars or passenger,
Floating like a mockery of its own purpose,
A mystery-ship worked loose by the rocking waves;
And I had to laugh as I saw it eke its route,
Bumping against the walls of the dark canal,
Stubbornly plying its cargo of water and leaves;
I had to laugh, by God, to keep from crying out.

Inscription For The Cairn Of An Archaic Indian Lying By The Strait Of Belle Isle

Seven thousand years have come and gone,
Seven thousand winters since the great white bear
Arose like a god of the ice he walked upon,
Heaving his bulk up into the dry crisp air
To learn if the breeze would willingly betray
Where the young hunter lay in wait with a spear,
Half-frozen in the scrub round the shore of the bay;
Uncertain manhood raging to quell its fear
As the fierce boy-killing god loped near.
Seven thousand years, neither man nor boy,
Since life last heard him laugh out loud
At the bird that answered his whittled toy,
The bird-bone flute that amused the cloud
Drifting down to summer like the ice of the sea;
For what man sings to his own father's rib
Like the silly bird chirping low in the tree?
Older than the dust of the widows of Sennacherib,
Seventy centuries locked in the cold crib
Of the planet's womb since he crouched and played
For his mother who scraped wet walrus hide,
Well-pleased with the male her magic made,
Splendid with love for the son who piped at her side.
But a boy found sleeping in a sandy grave,
Barely a man to tell by his crumbling teeth:
A creature free on a planet still naive,
Or the sacrifice of some early evil faith,
Some wolf-god howling out on the frozen heath
For the blood of the boy who played the bird-bone flute
And called to the pack with an eerie piercing trill
As the leader hushed and the pack fell mute
Beside the smoking carcass of another kill;
Or merely the victim of a virulent disease?
Seventy centuries keep their secrets well

That have kept this lone cairn's mysteries,
Seventy centuries that still refuse to tell
How this young Indian-Orpheus hunter fell
And was buried here beneath a slab of stone
Heaped up with boulders from a nearby creek.
What power could adolescent flesh put on
That a migrant tribe would stop to work a week
To inter a youth, his face turned north,
With a weight of stone upon his limber back
As if to insure he'd never rise again from earth
To finger the whistle hung from his boney neck,
Or mimic a bird for a summer cloud's sake?

On The Way To University

Now the snow comes down that all the morning fell
Half-heartless from the undecided sky
Like the harmless notions of a lonely damaged will
Expending itself in dreams it can't apply:

As if a galaxy were gradually undone,
And hosts of stars released to drift away,
Plump flakes obscure the custard-yellow sun
With an aimless, quiet, undistinguished grey;

And footprints that traversed the open field
Are worn down like ancient Nordic runes,
And acres where the wind had hoped to wield
An easy softness rounds the creases of the dunes.

At The Window

Venus glares through the black leafless maple boughs
And lifts me from myself, that brilliant light,
One stolen moment I stand and stare tonight,
Confused as never before, broken by vows
I made and could not keep for all my trying,
Diminished in my own eyes by my pride,
And sick, sick of the vague inward dying
Of the creature who would out to walk at my side.
Unlooked-for peace in just a simple sighting,
Though its rays are smeared by the pane's old glass,
Dear God, Guide, who has brought this light to pass,
Make an end of the creature I feel fighting
To be free of the trap I have tripped on its leg;
Dear sister planet, intercede for us I beg.

The Winter Morning Meditation Of The Poet-Janitor Of The Fifth Avenue Free Methodist Church

Who works the filigree upon the frozen panes,
Or lengthens water into icicles,
Or blows the rare crystal cranes
That sometimes stride the windowsills?
What vague notions shape to ice
When water grows implacable;
Does water listen to an inner voice;
Is this cold art its vocable?

God calls the sweeper to his broom,
Who steps into the freezing dawn,
Lost in the cloud of the white plume
His moist breath hangs a fancy on:
It's Sunday and the stairs must be
Swept of snow and chipped of ice
If he's to go on writing poetry
While the church-bells raise their iron voice.

Above Two Capitols

Fierce Sirius flashing in the eastern sky,
Orion rising over the towers of Ottawa:
Stars I learned by heart in green Victoria,
Though tempered there by ocean raised up high—
Soft veils of mist like netting on a tent
From time to time blown open to the eye
By cedar-scented winds from the Orient,
Pushing slow cloud-booms across the sky.
But here, now winter clears the upper air,
I seek the deeper dark the maples keep
In groves where the drunks will freeze in their sleep
Beside the drained canal, out of the city's glare;
I seek the deeper dark to see more clearly
Those high bright ministers burning merely.

Canadian Venus

Young couple kissing in the powdery snow
That gleams like brass in the noon light
And gathers in her chestnut hair
Without melting. One minute, two minutes;
It seems they are never going to stop.
He folds his hands behind his back,
Holding a white letter, as if to say
To anyone who might be watching:
I know this is a rather prolonged kiss
To be involved in here with her
While one by one the neighbours come to their windows to watch;
But what can I do?— She insists,
And I'm afraid she'll think there's something wrong
If I don't match her kiss for kiss. Ah, there,
It's done: now all the neighbours catch their breath
And turn back to their tedious winter lives
With a will renewed at least a little by these two
Who part and go their separate ways; he, only,
Looking back.

Upon An Old Photograph Of Myself

Someone better than I am, more full of hope,
If hope is any gauge to go by. In me
Is Adam once again condemned to cope,
Once more evicted for the old complicity.
Toil, death, need, a woman's scorn,
The doubt of self which is the worm to joy;
Is it human to curse the day we were born,
Life for the man to be less than the boy?
Weep; I have wept and exhausted tears;
So the rain leaves a window streaked with dirt.
Rage; I have been a fool beyond my years
And called that tragic which was only hurt.

In The Parking Lot

I smash my hand against the concrete wall,
Breaking my knuckles and wrist to deprive
Murder of the means to hit him again. I appall
Everyone who will not make the slightest move
To help him out, these souls who disapprove
Of violence so much they stand in thrall
Like puzzled sheep, or glare like impotence,
Until a shame much crueller than remorse
Wells up within me even drunk, and innocence
I see is no one they'll defend by force,
And holding out my left good hand to him, I nurse
The temper that must down the eisel of offense;
And ask him if he will forgive me just to show
The rest of them what he and I already know.

For Joanne In The Morning

You dream, and dreaming, turn
Within the fever's solitude;
Then call out names I scorn
And temper the loving mood
That prompts these words to you,
But only for a little while,
Since love is seldom true
That's never known the vile
Worm by which we tell
The live rose from maché
Or love from the bagatelle
Those earlier rivals weigh
Your life by even now
While I must watch and wait
More solemn than the vow
Of some poor Paraclete
Who trusts he's still your lover
And will try to stay awake
Sitting up late for either
His heart or your fever to break.

The Human Solstice

High in the lean maples, the winter sun,
I have watched it rise all morning,
Has set the icicles dripping one
By one like taps with worn washers;
And guilded puddles on the brown road gold.
Soon the children will be coming home for lunch,
Their cheeks and noses rouged with cold,
Their mittens wet, a bootlace snapped,
Nylon chafing nylon as they walk.
And there to meet them at the draughty door,
As each must ring or push or knock,
Should be someone so full of love,
This winter sun for all its cosmic touches,
Will shine with envy on the mended glove
I found and spread on the snowberry bushes.

The Premonition

The air is dazzled by the rising coils of snow
The wind skims off the last night's gentle fall.
Footprints are erased and over all
The wide pure plain of the park below
Little tines of light are winking at the sun.
Blue, the sky, with here and there a cloud
Banked high as if they too were ploughed
By graders shifting winter's slushy ton;
In short, a brisk, bright January day.
I am alive, inside, and at the windowpane,
In health, in love, and free of any chain
But those whose rattling is the sound of play:
Why, then, like a thief, do I still start to see
The saffron dog-stained snow ahead of me?

Existential Man, The Heredox

From another vantage, another time,
He'll say what he did
Was, afterall, correct:
"Nothing else I could do,"
He might admit with a shrug,
Half-recalling the argument
Or, laughing among friends,
Dining to his new success,
He just might confide
"It was the most difficult thing
I've ever had to do,"
And flush with regret
He'd never be able to do it again.
I can see, too, how
Given a little longer, another
Place to view the thought-bare
Time-honoured event, he might
Even rue it as a mistake
And begin to wonder
What he had lost
By making one, and not the other
Choice. By then, of course,
As a final complication,
He'll be allowed to know.

Skating At Night

All balanced upon a sharpened blade,
Stroke after stroke, accelerating through the dark,
Like time that is bound by the width of a swinging arc,
The body leans into each successive grade,
Forcing its muscles to fast-talk gravity
And free the mind awhile to flatter itself in flight.
Brueghel could have painted what I see here tonight,
One old man skating with perfect suavity
And pride because he tacks the easiest of all
Upon a surface where his grandson's twenty years
Overthrow their cargo like drunken mutineers
Trying to right their ship in a sudden squall;
And painted, too, the couple, arm in arm,
Who glide in marvellous unison over the luminous ice
Even as the one dwells upon the other's face,
Careless of the deep cracks that will not spoil their form.

The Marriage Of Heaven And Earth

Can mind haunt heaven here on earth;
What if, I ask, because I am a man,
Life house the seeds of another birth;
Death be but a false meridian?
I think of spirits pure as the heart of a flame,
Yet able to see, hear, touch, and feel,
Nothing lost of the world from which they came,
But spirits so scioned to the stock of the real
Life and knowledge grow a greater tree
When bodies fall like blossoms from the fruit.
And must I call this vision fantasy;
Over the coals of my mind walk barefoot
Only to hear I am greased with a trance?
I see angels, male and female, meet
And the one look upon the other's countenance,
As together at last in the bridal suite,
Heaven that made Earth an old widow
Lies down beside her a second, happier time,
And lifts the veil off years of lingering sorrow,
And holds her there forever in her prime.

An Attempt At Prayer

Lord, I am in love with your planet;
Life — I have not staled of your gift — is joy to me;
I love my wife and child and the flowers they bring with them;
I love the rain, sun, stars, the usual things
As though they had never been loved before;
I love them with an intensity that must surely
End in death, whether violent or natural departure,
And though I will not know if I have understood it right
Until, Lord, I am overwhelmed in the dark of you;
I have aspired to the wisdom of your words
For I know I am no thing more marvellous than they.
Lord, it is truly beautiful, this life,
And if you were to take it from me this very instant
I would yet have enough to dream on for all time
If that is what it will be given me to do
When I hope at last you're there to come to.
Like warm tears I must let have their way with me
Lord, you arc like the waters of a fountain
Through this small influence you have reared from the clay;
Lord, make me the garden you wait in;
I am yours for the musing, on a whim;
I am yours like something you may have forgotten.
If I have wandered, Lord, it is that you would find me,
For there is nothing I love so much Lord
As to see you take the slightest pleasure
In this dull work, me. I am yours if you would,
And even if you would not, I am yours;
One of the four billion of your imperfect versions,
I am content with that; I have been conceived
Which is more astounding than if I had not been,
Which is inconceivable. Lord, my achiever,
Like a straw in the mandible of a returning ant,
I am the little that mounds your laws like hills,
Nor are the stars more, nor the greatest thing,

Which is but a soil upon your drapery. Lord,
Break me like light into my constituents;
Show me up for all the human eye can see;
Lord, you have surpassed me like eternity;
I submit to you the lover's love of his plight;
I come to you in the trappings of that old Mortal, Anguish,
For this is all that has been given to me to wear
Amid your miracle, and Lord, it is enough.
Or scald me again at bright Hiroshima,
Or abase me even now in a room in Harlem,
Or play with me in the dollhouse at Treblinka,
Or keep me guessing in Rhodesia, Peking, Beirut,
And yet I will cling to you like an atmosphere.
For I am inevitably yours, O blessèd ransom,
Though I am lost to my abductors anyway,
It was never so much to me that you could save,
But that you wanted to. All praise to your visit,
Praise in the second millenium since your death;
This fond notion awaits you, Lord of my Revels;
I dream of you as a stricken country of its junta;
And though they take you down from the hospital wards
That I might not see depiction of your suffering
And so suffer; the wards are no happier without you;
Nor is your image less vivid in the impression
You have left upon the wall, as upon my mind,
For you have yet to fill all your galleries;
For your gentleness must yet be turned to whole milk,
For you have mastered me like a wayward planet,
For you are the random atom that initiates a world,
For you are dying like a child within my reach,
For you are the risk I have been trying to take,
For you qualify me like cadmium in a nuclear pile,
For I am confounded by the simplicity of your response,
For I will yield to you like the throat of a lover,
For you would forgive in me what others have learned to praise,
For I have met the criminal who is wiser than his judge,

For I have seen him grieve like beautifully tempered steel,
For I have learned to fail like an objective humanist,
For I have grown argumentative and sure of suffering,
For I have waited in the halls of worthless promotion,
For humans pick at the food between my teeth,
For I am living in a comfortable sort of hell,
For I have turned my back when it would have cost me nothing ,
For I have heard the useless, pampered women sigh like private schools,
For I have heard their husbands claim they earn what they enjoy,
For their children grow up with advantages,
For I have seen how their litmus turns only one colour,
For I have seen whom they select to keep on the kidney-machine,
For their priests bless the corpse as it drops through the trap,
For I have met a man who cannot read,
For I have met the poet who waited on tables,
For she must live off the bounty that drops to the floor,
For their teachers are specialized, passionless butts,
For their teachers are liberal, passionate butts,
For if you would be thought wise, think them wise,
For if you would have insight, praise their book,
For if you would marry their daughters, marry them,
For there is more understanding one by one,
For their fools take themselves seriously,
For only a pleonast can hold office,
For their doctors lobby against the general health,
For their scientists do not heed their own inventions,
For it offends everyone, so it offends no one,
For justice is meted out like a privilege,
For the greater thief goes free to write his book,
For evangelists would recommend castration,
For they work together in a factory,
For they have poisoned the bay where I used to swim,
For moths evolve the colour of soot,
For their athletes win the luxury car,
For reason is an unskilled occupation,

For they cry their goods in my living-room,
For excellence must have a wealthy pupil,
For the safest place to hide is in the army,
For age is lost like a star in the sun,
For youth is forced to accept its pension,
For evil's preferred if it proves efficient,
For beauty's mirror is smeared with offal,
For the last shall be last for the first are first,
Where to search for the truth is to toil for a jargon,
Where to draw a conclusion is simply to make an end.